ENGLISH

MARIGOLD

Emmanuel D'Souza
Gloria D'Souza

ARIHANT PRAKASHAN, MEERUT

WORKBOOK English 5th

Published by Arihant Prakashan, Meerut

ॐ **Administrative & Production Offices**

Regd. Office
'Ramchhaya' 4577/15, Agarwal Road, Darya Ganj, New Delhi -110002
Tele: 011- 47630600, 43518550; Fax: 011- 23280316

Head Office
Kalindi, TP Nagar, Meerut (UP) - 250002
Tel: 0121-2401479, 2512970, 4004199; Fax: 0121-2401648

ॐ **Sales & Support Offices**

Agra, Ahmedabad, Bengaluru, Bhubaneswar, Bareilly, Chennai, Delhi, Guwahati, Hyderabad, Jaipur, Jhansi, Kolkata, Lucknow, Meerut, Nagpur & Pune.

ॐ **ISBN** 978-93-11121-95-6

ॐ **Price** ₹ 80.00

Production Team

Publishing Manager
Keshav Mohan, Amit Verma

Project Head
Karishma Yadav

Project Coordinator
Aleena Zaidi

Project Editor
Amit Tanwar

Cover Designer
Shanu Mansoori

Inner Designer
Ravi Negi

DTP Operator
Ravindra Kumar

Proof Readers
Kiran, Esha, Soniya

For further information about the books published by Arihant, log on to **www.arihantbooks.com** or e-mail at info@arihantbooks.com

Workbook, Why?

"Knowledge will not be with you for Long Unless You Practice"

This quotation answer the above question 'Workbook, Why ?'
perfectly, i.e Workbooks are made to give the students practice required to achieve
perfection and mastery in the subject. These are the only Workbooks, which are strictly
based on **NCERT, the only recommended books by Govt. of India & CBSE**
(reference Circular No. Acad-41/2015 dated 20th July 2015).

Given below is the detailed description of Workbook and some of its special features

ONLY COMPLETE WORKBOOK BASED ON NCERT

NCERT textbooks are the only textbooks, which have been prepared according to
National Curriculum Framework, which discourages the idea of rote learning rather
focus on inculcating creativity & initiative in the students to make them participants in
learning not just a receiver of a one-way communication.

Keeping the importance of NCERT textbooks in mind we have prepared this Workbook,
strictly based on NCERT content, this Workbook will complement NCERT by providing
practice on the material given in each chapter of NCERT textbook. This is the only
Workbook, which covers complete Syllabus of English. It has all the four sections;
Literature, Grammar, Writing and **Reading**.

WORKBOOK- PURPOSE, USE & FEATURES

This Workbook, through its **numerous exercises** having different **variety of
questions** covering **practical importance** of English & **Day-to-Day
communication**, will prove to be **equally useful** for both, **Classroom** and **at Home**.
One more purpose of this Workbook is to provide the students a **systematic practice**
of the content taught in the class and what they study in the textbooks.

Some special features of this workbook are

- Complete coverage of all the Sections; Literature, Grammar, Writing and Reading

- Complete coverage of all the Chapters of the NCERT Textbook

- Different variety of questions; Fill in the Blanks, True-False, Matching, Multiple
  Choice Questions, Differentiate between, Define the following, One word for, Odd
  One Out, Very Short Answer, Short Answer, Long Answer Type etc.

WORKBOOK-DESIGNED TO IMPROVE SUBJECT ABILITIES

All the material given in this workbook is tailored to suit subject content with equal
support on learning, which will surely help students to boost their abilities and
confidence in the subject.

*I look forward for the feedback from students, teachers and parents for the further improvement of
the contents of this book. I will try to update the contents according to your feedback in further
editions of this Workbook.*

The Publisher

Contents

SECTION A   Literature

SECTION B   Grammar

SECTION C   Writing

SECTION D   Reading Comprehension

[Chapter **1**]

Ice-Cream Man *Rachel Field*

Text Based Questions

1. State 'T' for true and 'F' for false statements.

(i) The ice-cream man comes at a lightning speed.

(ii) There is an umbrella above the cart.

(iii) The sight around the ice-cream cart is sad.

2. Read the following lines of the poem and answer the questions that follow.

> Beneath his round umbrella,
> Oh, what a joyful sight,
> To see him fill the cones with mounds
> Of cooling brown and white

(i) To whom does 'his' refer to in the given lines?

(ii) What is a joyful sight for children?

(iii) Find the word from the stanza which means the same as 'sight'?

(a) Find   (b) Obstruct

(c) View   (d) Glimpse

Very Short Answer Type Questions

3. Where does the ice-cream man keep his stuff?

4. In what way do the children cluster around the ice-cream man?

Short Answer Type Questions

5. What all does the ice-cream man carry?

6. Which flavours of ice-cream are mentioned in the poem?

7. Why is the cart of the ice-cream man compared to a flower-bed?

Language Based Questions

1. Match the following words to their meanings.

Column A	Column B
(i) Trundle	(a) Pile
(ii) Cluster	(b) Move slowly
(iii) Blaze	(c) Gather around
(iv) Mound	(d) Bright flame

2. Make sentences from the following words.

   (i) Bed

   (ii) Cones

   (iii) Cart

3. List a few words that rhyme with the following words.

   (i) Round

   (ii) Sight

   (iii) Heat

4. Write any three mm, oo, ll, rr, tt, ee words in the spaces given below. For hint, one of each of the type is done for you.

   (i) Su**mm**er

   (ii) C**oo**ling

   (iii) Vani**ll**a

Wonderful Waste!

Text Based Questions

1. State 'T' for true and 'F' for false statements.
   (i) The cook ordered a feast for the Maharaja.
   (ii) Avial became famous all over Kerala.
   (iii) Nobody wanted to know the name of the new dish.
   (iv) The Maharaja entered the kitchen to survey the dishes.

2. Read the following lines of the poem and answer the questions that follow.

> Then he cut them into long strips.
> He put them in a huge pot and
> placed it on the fire to cook.

   (i) Who is 'He' in the above lines?

   ____

   (ii) What was cut into long strips?

   ____

   (iii) Find two adjectives and two verbs from the above lines.

   Adjectives ____________________   ____________________

   Verbs ____________________   ____________________

Very Short Answer Type Questions

3. Why was the cook in a fix?

   ____

4. How was the name of the new dish pronounced as?

   ____

Short Answer Type Questions

5. How did the cook react to the Maharaja's order?

6. Why was everyone eager to know the name of the dish?

Long Answer Type Question

7. Describe in detail how the new dish (avial) was prepared.

Language Based Questions

1. Match the following words and phrases with their meanings.

Column A		Column B	
(i)	Lo and behold	(a)	Hearty meal for many guests
(ii)	In a fix	(b)	Waste
(iii)	Scrap	(c)	A difficult situation
(iv)	Feast	(d)	What a surprise!

2. List any five things that are needed to make a dish. The first one has been filled for you.

(i) _Water_   (ii) ___________   (iii) ___________

(iv) ___________   (v) ___________   (vi) ___________

3. A few words are listed below.

Tempting	*Travancore*	*Surveyed*	*Huge*	*Feast*
Long	*Cooked*	*Kerala*	*Cleaned*	*Avial*

(i) Pick out the nouns from the list. ________________________________

(ii) Pick out the verbs from the list. ________________________________

(iii) Pick out the adjectives from the list. ________________________________

4. Describe any two ways in which you can cut down wastage of: water, electricity, paper.

Saving Water

(i) ____

(ii) ____

Saving Electricity

(i) ____

(ii) ____

Saving Paper

(i) ____

(ii) ____

5. Describe in your words a feast that you have attended.

Complete the description by keeping in mind the following points.

- Occasion of the feast
- Venue
- Number of guests (Approximately)
- Details of dishes and desserts served
- Who all from your family attended the feast?
- How did you prepare/what did you wear etc?
- What you enjoyed the most e.g. dance, food, games, ceremony etc?

____

____

____

____

Bamboo Curry *A Santhal Folk Tale*

Text Based Questions

1. State 'T' for true and 'F' for false statements.

   (i) The root of the bamboo is cooked and eaten.

  (ii) The mother-in-law of the bridegroom cooked a special dish for him.

 (iii) The dish made by the mother-in-law was tasteless.

 (iv) The bridegroom chopped the bamboo.

Very Short Answer Type Questions

2. What kind of folk tale is 'Bamboo Curry'?

3. Who carried the bamboo door with him?

Short Answer Type Questions

4. Why was bridegroom's wife shocked when he asked her to make curry out of the bamboo door?

5. What did the bridegroom's in-laws say to him, when they came to visit the young couple?

Long Answer Type Question

6. How did the new couple try to prepare the bamboo curry? Describe in detail.

Language Based Questions

1. Match the following words in the rectangular boxes with their opposites in the round boxes.

(i) Special   (a) Soft

(ii) Foolish   (b) Subtract

(iii) Hard   (c) Usual

(iv) Add   (d) Wise

2. Make sentences from the following words.

(i) Too _______________   (ii) Shocked _______________

(iii) Visit _______________   (iv) Laugh _______________

(v) Hard _______________

3. Write two words in the cloud that rhyme the same as the one mentioned in the cloud.

hard   curry   bamboo

shoot   chopping

4. List the name of two plants whose leaves you use in cooking. Also list the reason for using them in your dishes.

(*You may take help of your mother for completing this exercise*)

Name of the plant	Reason for using its leaves
(i) _______________	_______________
(ii) _______________	_______________

[Chapter **1**]

Teamwork   *Jan Nigro*

Text Based Questions

1. State 'T' for true and 'F' for false statements.

(i) There are many advantages of teamwork.

(ii) A 'you' or a 'me' becomes an us in a team.

(iii) It is sad to shoot the basketball through the hoop.

2. Read the following lines of the poem and answer the questions that follow.

> Sometimes it can be a big plus,
> When a you or a me becomes an us!

(i) Describe what is meant by 'big plus'.

____

(ii) The word 'us' in the above line relates to a

(a) beam   (b) cream

(c) team   (d) neem

(iii) Find three pronouns from the lines.

_______ _______ _______

Very Short Answer Type Questions

3. How can we make our dream work?

____

4. List the two games mentioned in the poem.

____

Short Answer Type Questions

5. List any three advantages of teamwork.

   (i) ____

   (ii) ____

   (iii) ____

6. What would happen if nobody makes a pass in the game of basketball?

____

Language Based Questions

1. Match the following with their correct meanings.

Column A	Column B
(i) Passes	(a) Advantage
(ii) Baton	(b) Move onward
(iii) Hoop	(c) Short tube or stick
(iv) Plus	(d) A wooden or iron ring

2. Make sentences from the following words.

   (i) Joy ____

   (ii) Baton ____

   (iii) Goal ____

   (iv) Share ____

3. List two words that rhyme the same as

   (i) Goal _______________   _______________

   (ii) Hoop _______________   _______________

   (iii) Plus _______________   _______________

   (iv) Dream _______________   _______________

4. Fill the letters to complete the names of some commonly played games.

(i) H _ C _ _ Y   (ii) G _ _ F

(iii) C _ _ C _ E _   (iv) L _ D _

(v) C _ _ S _

5. Name the game shown in the picture below. Describe how it is played.

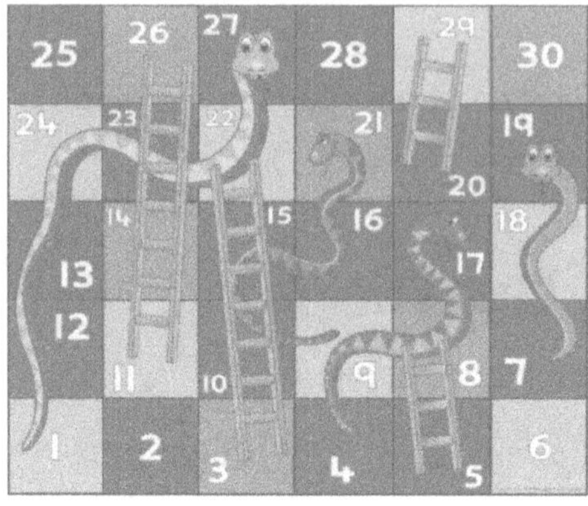

Name of the Game

Method of Playing

6. Describe a game that you played as being part of a team. Keep the following points in mind while describing it.

- Name of the game
- Venue of the game
- Did you enjoy playing the game?
- Number of players in each team
- Role played by you in the team

7. Describe 'relay race' in your own words.

Flying Together   *Shiv Kumar*

Text Based Questions

1. State 'T' for true and 'F' for false statements.

(i) The tree was located in a park.

(ii) The creeper was located at the foot of the tree.

(iii) The geese destroyed the creeper.

(iv) The hunter trapped the geese in his net.

2. Read the following lines of the story and answer the questions that follow.

In the evening, the geese returned home.
They did not notice the net. As they flew into the tree, they were trapped.

(i) When did the geese return home?

____

(ii) Who are 'they' in the above lines?

____

(iii) Find one pronoun and two nouns from the lines.

Pronoun _________________   Nouns _________________ _________________

Very Short Answer Type Questions

3. Who came to catch the geese?

____

4. Did the geese notice the net?

____

Short Answer Type Questions

5. How did the geese get trapped in the net?

6. What did the old bird warn the other geese about?

Long Answer Type Question

7. How did the geese escape from the hunter's trap?

Language Based Questions

1. Identify the adjectives in the following sentences and give their opposites

   (i) There stood a very tall tree.   Adjective ________ Opposite ________

   (ii) This is a small creeper.   Adjective ________ Opposite ________

   (iii) "Don't you see?" replied the wise bird.   Adjective ________ Opposite ________

2. Add the correct prefix to the words given in the bracket and complete the following.

(im) (re) (un) (dis)

  (i) This water is _________ (pure).

  (ii) The coolie _________ (loaded) the luggage.

  (iii) Sohini had to _________ (write) the assignment.

3. Colour the cloud which has rhyming words in it.

Dig Fig Big	Clump Jump Fear	Zoom Loom Broom	Strong Belong Zone	Scum Rum Bum

4. Write the singular form of the following words.

Words	Singular Form	Words	Singular Form
(i) Geese		(v) Cacti	
(ii) Hunters		(vi) Halves	
(iii) Mice		(vii) Lives	
(iv) Flies		(viii) Fungi	

[Chapter **1**]

My Shadow   *Robert Louis Stevenson*

Text Based Questions

1. State 'T' for true and 'F' for false statements.

(i) The shadow is compared to a ghost.

(ii) The poet finds the way a shadow grows as funny.

(iii) Buttercup is the name of an ice-cream.

(iv) The poet finds his shadow similar to him.

(v) The little shadow goes up and down with me.

2. Read the following lines of the poem and answer the questions that follow.

The funniest thing about him is the way he likes to grow,
Not at all like proper children which is always very slow.

(i) Who is 'he' in the above lines?

____

(ii) What is the funniest thing about 'he'?

____

(iii) Complete the series.

(a) ____________, funnier, funniest

(b) Slow, ____________, slowest

Very Short Answer Type Questions

3. What follows us whenever there is light?

____

4. What does the poet mean by India-rubber ball?

____

Short Answer Type Questions

5. How does the shadow like to grow?

6. At what time of the day is your shadow lazy? Why?

Language Based Questions

1. Match the following with their meanings.

Column A	Column B
(i) Buttercup	(a) Bad
(ii) Arrant	(b) A yellow flower
(iii) Dawn	(c) Period of partial darkness between day and night
(iv) Dusk	(d) The first appearance of daylight in the morning

2. Identify the misspelled words from the following and spell them correctly.

> *heales, shadow, propar, topaz, deew, earely, arrant, follew*

There are _____________ misspelled words.

Their correct spellings are ___________ ___________ ___________ ___________

3. Make sentences from the following words.

(i) Shadow _________________________ (ii) Jump_______________________

(iii) Children_________________________

4. Have you ever been afraid of your shadow? Perhaps, at night or when you were alone. Describe such an incident in your own words.

Robinson Crusoe Discovers a Footprint

Adapted from Daniel Defoe's Robinson Crusoe

Text Based Questions

1. State 'T' for true and 'F' for false statements.

   (i) There were many footprints on the sand.

   (ii) Robinson was very frightened to see the footprint.

   (iii) He ran for cover, faster than any animal could run.

   (iv) He ran away from the island to save his life.

2. Read the following lines of the story and answer the questions that follow.

> I did not sleep that night. The more I
> thought about what I had seen, the more
> afraid I became.

   (i) Why did Robinson not sleep that night?

   ____

   (ii) Find two verbs from the above lines.

   ____

   (iii) Write down the superlative form of afraid.

   ____

Very Short Answer Type Questions

3. What did Robinson call his cave?

4. What did Robinson think when he placed his foot alongside the footprint?

Short Answer Type Questions

5. Why was Robinson afraid of the footprint?

6. Why did Robinson run inside his cave?

Long Answer Type Question

7. What two things made Robinson realise that it was not his footprint?

Language Based Questions

1. Match the following with their meanings.

	Column A		Column B
(i)	Savage	(a)	Confident
(ii)	Wander	(b)	Wild people
(iii)	Bold	(c)	Go from place to place

2. Find the words from the chapter which mean the following. The first letter of the word has been filled for you.

   (i) To become afraid   F _______

   (ii) Being followed by someone   C _______

3. One day you move out of your house and see strange animal footprints in your garden. How will you find out which animal left those footprint? It could be a dog, cat, goat or even a jackal! What will you do?

[Chapter 1]
Crying   *Galway Kinnell*

Text Based Questions

1. State 'T' for true and 'F' for false statements.

   (i) You must cry until your bedsheet is soaked.

   (ii) After crying, you should throw open your doors.

   (iii) You should sing "Ha!Ha" when people ask you what's going on.

   (iv) Happiness hides in the last tear.

Very Short Answer Type Questions

2. According to the poet, what is of no use?

3. What should we do after crying a lot?

Short Answer Type Questions

4. As per the poet, what should you do in the shower?

5. What two moods are mentioned in the poem?

Language Based Questions

1. Identify the words from the poem which are the opposites of

  (i) Close _________________________   (ii) Down _________________________

  (iii) First _________________________   (iv) Sadness _________________________

  (v) Misuse _________________________

2. The following words taken from the poem are jumbled. Rearrange the letters to form meaningful words.

  (i) LASPHS _________________________   (ii) WORHT _________________________

  (iii) POELPE _________________________   (iv) WILLPO _________________________

  (v) SUMT _________________________

3. Write two words in the balloon that rhyme with the one mentioned in it.

| pillow | tear | cry | jump |

4. Identify the misspelled words from the words listed in the box.

| happiness | gross | followw | threw |
| pouder | clown | shoping | blouse |

There are ___________ misspelled words.

Their correct spellings are

(i) ___________   (ii) ___________   (iii) ___________   (iv) ___________

5. The expression Ha!Ha!Ha Ha! signifies happiness or a happy mood. There are other expressions which convey different moods. Given below are a few of them. Match them with their corresponding mood.

(i) Ahh!	(a) Triumph
(ii) Oops!	(b) Disgust
(iii) Ughh.....	(c) Fault/Error
(iv) Hurrah!	(d) Delight

My Elder Brother

Text Based Questions

1. State 'T' for true and 'F' for false statements.

   (i) Both the brothers lived at their home.

   (ii) Bhaiya was younger to Munna.

   (iii) Munna wanted to go home.

   (iv) Bhaiya was a meritorious student.

   (v) Munna liked to fly kites.

2. Read the following passage and answer the questions that follow.

The results were out once again and it so happened that Munna passed and Bhaiya failed again. Bhaiya was really upset. Munna was also sad seeing his brother so unhappy. Bhaiya now becomes gentler with Munna. Munna became naughtier because of this and studied even less than before.

   (i) What was the result?

   (ii) Why was Munna sad?

   (iii) Munna became naughtier. Why?

   (iv) Find opposites of the following words from the passage.

      (a) Happy _____________   (b) More _____________

      (c) After _____________

Very Short Answer Type Questions

3. From which language has the story been translated?

4. What was the topic on which Bhaiya was asked to write a short essay?

Short Answer Type Questions

5. What all games did Munna like to play?

6. Why Munna had tears in his eyes?

Long Answer Type Questions

7. Why did Bhaiya scold Munna and how?

8. What lesson does the chapter teach you?

Language Based Questions

1. Make sentences from the following words.

    (i) Experience

    (ii) Upset

    (iii) Rush

    (iv) Ashamed

    (v) Scary

2. Write the opposite of the words given below by using the prefixes dis, un, im. The first one has been done for you.

	Word	Opposite
(i)	Polite	Impolite
(ii)	Important	
(iii)	Punctual	
(iv)	Obedient	
(v)	Honour	
(vi)	Happy	
(vii)	Proper	

3. Match the following words with their meanings.

Column A	Column B
(i) Ashamed	(a) To hurry
(ii) Scary	(b) Like
(iii) Rush	(c) Fearsome
(iv) Breeze	(d) To feel shameful
(v) Prefer	(e) A gentle wind

4. Build the ladder by making words starting with S.

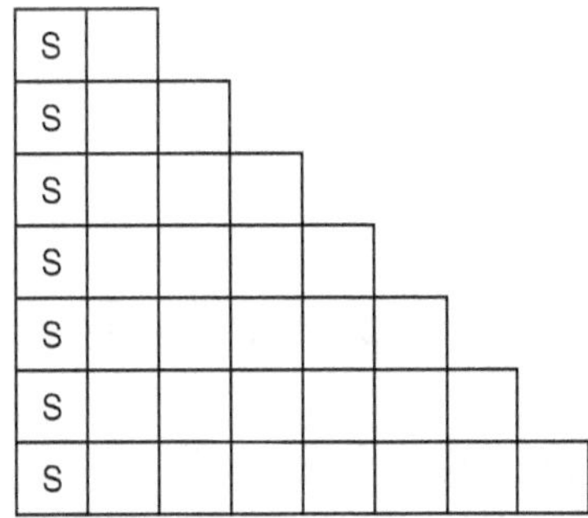

5. Suppose you are Munna and you want to pen down your feeling for Bhaiya in your diary entry. What will you write? Express your views in the space given below.

[Chapter **1**]

The Lazy Frog

Text Based Questions

1. State 'T' for true and 'F' for false statements.

  (i) The name of the frog is TED.

  (ii) The frog's mother needs his help.

  (iii) The frog shows respect to the lady frogs who are passing by him.

  (iv) The frog works throughout the day.

2. Read the following extract of the poem and answer the questions that follow.

> To move two inches, much preferring
> To be extremely hard-of-hearing.
> He lies there in a silent heap,
> And stays conveniently asleep.

  (i) Who is 'He' in the above lines?

____

  (ii) What does 'He' do while laying?

____

  (iii) Which word or phrase in the above passage means 'deaf'? _______________

Very Short Answer Type Questions

3. Where does the frog loll all day?

____

4. How is the frog described in the poem?

____

Short Answer Type Questions

5. How does the frog react when his mother calls him?

____

6. What happens when a lady frog passes by Fred?

____

Language Based Questions

1. Circle the correctly spelled words from the following.

	A	B	C
(i)	Extremly	Extremely	Extrimely
(ii)	Prefering	Preffering	Preferring
(iii)	Bothar	Bother	Bather

2. Do as directed.

(i) Select an adjective from the first line of the poem _______________ .

(ii) Select an adjective from the fifth line of the poem _______________ .

(iii) Select a pronoun from the last line of the poem _______________ .

3. Complete the cloud by filling in two rhyming words which rhyme with the one mentioned in the cloud.

4. Select the odd one from the following.

(i) Cow, Horse, Shoes, Goat, Pig _______________

(ii) Hand, Legs, Mouth, Fear, Ears _______________

(iii) Rose, Marigold, Tulip, Lotus, Frog _______________

Rip Van Winkle

Adapted from The Legend of Rip Van Winkle Washington Irving

Text Based Questions

1. State 'T' for true and 'F' for false statements.

  (i) The only problem with Rip was that he was hyper-active.

  (ii) Rip used to play with children.

  (iii) The old man did not sport a beard.

  (iv) Rip drank the contents of the barrel.

  (v) Rip's farm was well-maintained.

2. Read the following lines of the story and answer the questions that follow.
He looked around for Wolf, but he was nowhere.
Rip whistled for him. "Wolf! Wolf!" he then shouted. No dog was to be seen.

  (i) Who is he in the above lines?

  ____

  (ii) Wolf was the name of _____________________ .

  (iii) Find two verbs from the lines. _______________   _______________

  (iv) Find two pronouns from the lines. _______________   _______________

Very Short Answer Type Questions

3. Where was Rip's village located?

____

4. Who was Rip's constant companion?

____

5. From where this story has been adapted?

____

Short Answer Type Questions

6. Why did the children like Rip?

7. Describe the appearance of the old man who asked Rip to carry the barrel.

8. Why did Rip obey the old man?

Long Answer Type Questions

9. Describe the condition of Rip's farm.

10. How and when did Rip realise that he had grown old?

Language Based Questions

1. Write the appropriate word by using the clues.

   (i) Wild unwanted plants   W _ _ D _

   (ii) Lines or folds on skin   _ R _ _ K _ E _

   (iii) Dreaming while awake   _ _ Y _ R _ _ M

   (iv) To climb down   D _ _ C _ N _

   (v) A wooden container for storing oil etc   _ A _ _ _ _

2. Listed below are a few words from the chapter that have been jumbled. Find the right word by unscrambling them.

   (i) GEIVLLA _____________   (ii) SELBMAR _____________

   (iii) DEOECH _____________   (iv) BURBED _____________

[Chapter **1**]

Class Discussion
Gervase Phinn

Text Based Questions

1. State 'T' for true and 'F' for false statements.

   (i) Jane participated in the class discussion.

   (ii) Jane spoke loudly.

   (iii) The teacher asked Jane as why she was quiet.

   (iv) Other students in the class were also silent.

   (v) Jane explained that as she was unwell so she did not feel like participating in the discussion.

2. Read the following extract and answer the questions that follow.

> "There are many people in this world.
> Who are rather quiet you know!"

   (i) Who said the above line?

   (ii) Why do you think she said so?

   (iii) Write the opposite of 'quiet'.

Very Short Answer Type Questions

3. Who aired their opinion in the discussion?

4. Why did the teacher ask Jane to 'please be plain'?

Short Answer Type Questions

5. Describe Jane's behaviour during the class discussion.

6. What reason was given by Jane to her teacher for not participating in the discussion?

Language Based Questions

1. Make sentences from the following words.

    (i) Plain

    (ii) Stare

    (iii) Quiet

    (iv) Barely

    (v) Surrounded

2. Match the following words in Column A with their meanings in Column B.

Column A	Column B
(i) Surround	(a) Barely, rarely
(ii) Chatter	(b) Issue or problem
(iii) Matter	(c) Enclose, circle
(iv) Hardly	(d) Informal talk

3. List two rhyming words in the balloons that sound similar to the one mentioned in it.

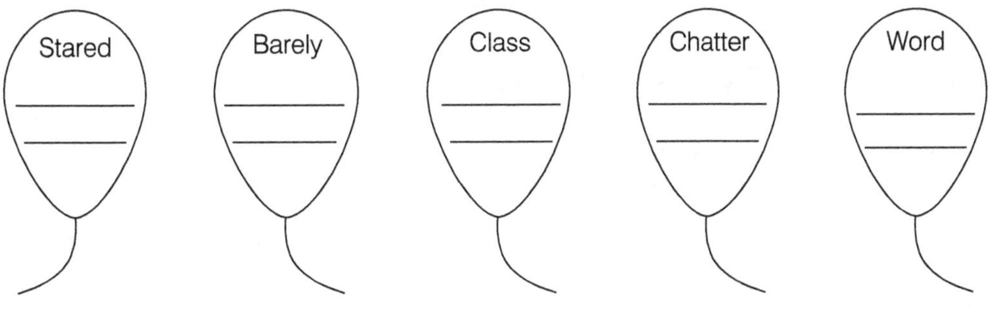

The Talkative Barber

From Arabian Nights

Text Based Questions

1. State 'T' for true and 'F' for false statements.

   (i) The barber was the eldest in his family.

  (ii) The barber was a chatter-box.

 (iii) The barber had five brothers.

 (iv) The Sultan was giving a feast to some friends at noon.

  (v) The barber was given three pieces of gold.

2. Read the following line and answer the questions that follow.
He then began narrating another story, which lasted half an hour.

   (i) Who is 'he' in the above line?

  (ii) Whom did 'he' narrate the story to?

 (iii) How many minutes does half an hour equal to?

 (iv) Find a verb and noun from the line.

Verb __________________________ Noun __________________________

Very Short Answer Type Questions

3. From where has this story been taken?

4. Which city did the barber live in?

Short Answer Type Questions

5. What reason was given by the barber for not leaving the Sultan's house?

6. Why was the barber keen to know about the Sultan's affair?

Long Answer Type Questions

7. How did the barber defend himself when the Sultan called him a chatterer?

8. Although the food was good, why do you think the barber asked for some fruits also for dessert?

Language Based Questions

1. Identify and encircle tho correctly spelled words from the following.

	A	B	C
(i)	Exhaust	Exhost	Exhest
(ii)	Satisfyd	Satisfieed	Satisfied
(iii)	Exclemed	Exclaimed	Exclamed
(iv)	Chaterer	Chaterrer	Chatterer
(v)	Speeches	Speches	Speaches

2. Do as directed.

(i) Find two words from the chapter that end in 'ly'

(ii) Find two words from the chapter that end in 'er'

(iii) Find one word from the chapter that ends in 'ous'

(iv) Find two words from the chapter that end with 'ing'

(v) Find two words from the chapter that end with 'st'

[Chapter 1]

Topsy-Turvy Land *HE Wilkinson*

Text Based Questions

1. State 'T' for true and 'F' for false statements.

   (i) The people wear shoes in their hands in the Topsy-Turvy Land.

   (ii) The boats travel on roads.

   (iii) You always get the things for which you have made the payment.

   (iv) The sea is made of sand and ketchup.

   (v) The front-door is located at the back of the houses.

2. Read the following stanza of the poem and answer the questions that follow.

     And buses on the sea you'll meet,
     While pleasure boats are planned,
     To travel up and down the streets
     Of Topsy-Turvy Land.

   (i) In Topsy-Turvy Land, how will one travel through sea?

   (ii) What are boats planned for?

   (iii) Find two nouns from the extract.

   (iv) Find two verbs from the extract.

Very Short Answer Type Questions

3. When do the children go to school in the Topsy-Turvy Land?

4. What must be grand in the Topsy-Turvy Land?

Short Answer Type Questions

5. List three things that are unusual about Topsy-Turvy Land from the first stanza of the poem.

6. Why Topsy-Turvy Land is referred to as an Upside-Down Land?

Language Based Questions

1. Find out the words from the poem that mean the following.

   (i) Big

   (ii) Feeling of enjoyment

   (iii) A large water body

   (iv) Go from one place to another

2. Write two words in the balloon that rhyme with the one mentioned in it.

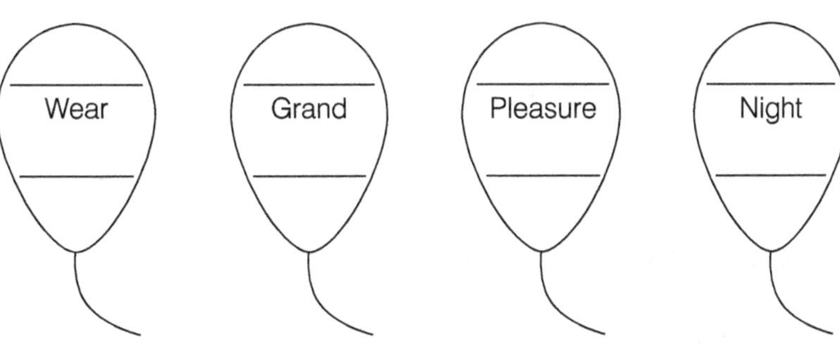

3. Pick the odd one out from the following.

   (i) Head, Feet, Hand, Grand, Leg

   (ii) Hat, Mat, Bat, Street, Fat

   (iii) Street, Tweet, Meet, Beat, Greet

   (iv) Chair, Stool, Table, Thermometer, Bed

Gulliver's Travels

Adapted from Jonathan Swift's (Gulliver's Travels)

Text Based Questions

1. State 'T' for true and 'F' for false statements.

    (i) The monster was able to overtake the speeding boat.

    (ii) The creature picked Gulliver and brought him close to his eyes.

    (iii) The cat was twenty times larger than an ox.

    (iv) Gulliver tried to speak to them loudly in several languages.

    (v) The farmer's wife was very cruel.

2. Read the lines of the story and answer the questions that follow.

They all sat on the ground to take a good look at me. I walked slowly backward and forward.

    (i) Who are 'they' in the above line?

    (ii) Why did they wanted to take a good look of Gulliver?

    (iii) Find one verb and one adverb from the lines.

    Verb _______________________   Adverb _______________________

Very Short Answer Type Questions

3. From which book has this story been taken?

4. Who was the author of that book?

Short Answer Type Questions

5. Why did Gulliver try to speak to the giants in several languages?

6. How did the farmers in the field react on seeing Gulliver?

Long Answer Type Questions

7. What difficulties did Gulliver face when he reached the barren and rocky country?

8. How was Gulliver's dinner at the farmer's house?

Language Based Questions

1. Find out the words from the chapter that have the following meaning.

(i) A land with no vegetation _______   (ii) A garment worn while cooking _______

(iii) To find new things _______   (iv) To shout very loudly _______

2. The word 'overtake' is formed by joining words 'over' and 'take'. Find three other words that start with 'over'. Also mention their meanings.

	Word	Meaning
(i)	_______	_______
(ii)	_______	_______
(iii)	_______	_______

3. List the opposite of the underlined words in the following sentences.

(i) The hill is very steep.   (ii) This portion of land is barren.

Opposite _______   Opposite _______

(iii) Is it possible to predict the future?   (iv) He spoke harshly.

Opposite _______   Opposite _______

Nobody's Friend   *Enid Blyton*

Text Based Questions

1. State 'T' for true and 'F' for false statements.

(i) The girl in the first stanza of the poem did not like to share her sweets.

(ii) One child wanted to share stuff with others in the poem.

(iii) The boy in the poem liked to share his tricycle.

(iv) The boy in the poem is everybody's friend.

(v) In the last stanza of the poem, the girl wanted to borrow things from others.

2. Read the following lines of the poem and answer the questions that follow.

> He had some toffee, and ate every bit,
> He had a tricycle he wouldn't lend.

(i) Why wouldn't 'He' share his things with others?

____

(ii) What did 'He' eat every bit?

____

(iii) Find nouns from the lines.

____

(iv) Find a pronoun from the lines.

____

(v) Write down the plural form of the following words.

(a) toffee ___________   (b) tricycle ___________

Very Short Answer Type Questions

3. What is meant by the phrase 'ate every bit' in the poem?

4. How many characters are there in the poem?

Short Answer Type Questions

5. List the things that the boy had with him.

6. Who is nobody's friend?

7. What all eatables did the girl in the last stanza have?

Language Based Questions

1. Circle the odd one.

  (i) lend, give, donate, take   (ii) share, bell, care, dare

  (iii) friend, buddy, chum, enemy   (iv) lend, wind, bend, send

2. Complete the words by using the given clues.

  (i) A three letter word which is the opposite of 'Friend' is: F _ _

  (ii) A 'Toffee' can also be called as a: S _ _ E _

  (iii) A cycle with two tyres is a :   B _ C _ C _E

  (iv) The opposite of 'Nobody' is: _ O _ _ B _ _ Y

  (v) A shop which sells sweets and chocolates is called as a   C _ N _ _ C _ I _ _ _ R _

3. Mention the things that you won't like to share with anyone. Also mention the reason for not sharing them.

The Little Bully

By Enid Blyton (Adapted)

Text Based Questions

1. State 'T' for true and 'F' for false statements.

   (i) Hari used to tease everyone in the class.

   (ii) Hari made friends with the monster crab.

   (iii) Nobody hated Hari.

   (iv) The lobster was the cousin of the giant crab.

   (v) Hari enjoyed the picnic.

2. Read the following line and answer the questions that follow.

"They only did to me what I keep doing to the other children," he thought.

   (i) Who is 'he' in the above line?

   ____

   (ii) What was done to him and by whom?

   ____

   (iii) What did 'he' used to do with other children?

   ____

   (iv) Find one noun and one pronoun from the line.

     (a) Noun _____________   (b) Pronoun _____________

Very Short Answer Type Questions

3. Why were all the children excited?

____

4. What did Hari do when he was angry on the picnic day?

____

Short Answer Type Questions

5. What two things did Hari do to tease others?

6. Why was pinching Hari no good?

7. What did Hari get for lunch for the picnic?

Long Answer Type Question

8. How did Hari realise his mistake?

Language Based Questions

1. Fill the boxes with the opposites of the words given in them.

(i) push   (ii) wild   (iii) excited   (iv) hoarse   (v) praise

2. Make sentences from the following words.

  (i) Bruise

 (ii) Nipped

(iii) Queer

3. Encircle the words from the following which are correctly spelled.

	A	B	C
(i)	Lept	Leapt	Laept
(ii)	Horid	Horidd	Horrid
(iii)	Pincer	Pinser	Pencer
(iv)	Stelk	Stalk	Stak

4. Suppose you are Hari. Write a diary entry on his behalf expressing a day of picnic.

[Chapter **1**]

Sing a Song of People

Lois Lbnski

Text Based Questions

1. State 'T' for true and 'F' for false statements.

   (i) The poem describes life in a town.

   (ii) There are eight stanzas in the poem.

   (iii) The people in the poem are in a hurry.

   (iv) Some people in the poem are also in the train.

2. Read the following lines of the poem and answer the questions that follow.

> People with their hats on,
> Going in the doors,
> People with umbrellas
> When it rains and pours.

   (i) Who all are going in the doors?

   (ii) What do people do, when it rains?

   (iii) What is meaning of the word 'pours'?

Very Short Answer Type Questions

3. Where is the subway?

4. What are grumpy people doing?

Short Answer Type Questions

5. What all places are mentioned in the poem?

6. How do people enjoy when they ride taxis?

7. How do people enter the tall buildings and stores?

8. What all kinds of people are mentioned in the poem?

Language Based Questions

1. Match the following with their meanings.

Column A	Column B
(i) Grumpy	(a) Below
(ii) Subway	(b) Footpath
(iii) Sidewalk	(c) Bad-tempered
(iv) Elevator	(d) An underground passage
(v) Underneath	(e) Lift

2. Write two words in the balloons that rhyme with the one mentioned in it.

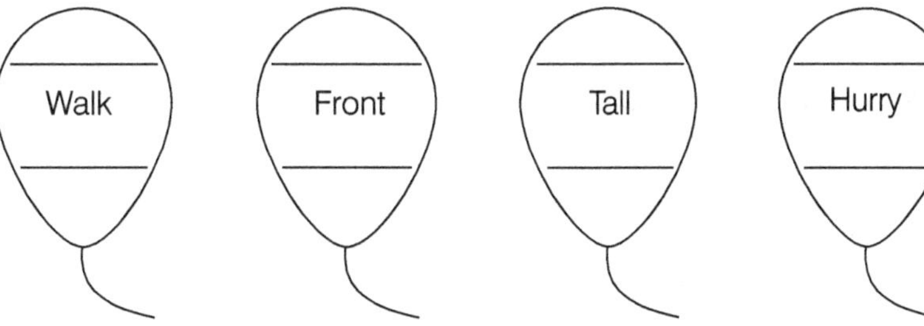

Around the World   *Jules Verne*

Text Based Questions

1. State 'T' for true and 'F' for false statements.

   (i) A herd of cows stopped the train.

   (ii) The bridge crashed after the train passed through the Medicine river.

   (iii) The train would go from the Atlantic to the Pacific Ocean.

   (iv) The train was attacked by hundreds of Sioux Indians.

   (v) Some of the travellers had rifles.

2. Read the following lines and answer the questions that follow.

The train headed for the steep mountains. This was the
most difficult part of the journey with its winding roads.

   (i) Why was this part the most difficult part of the journey?

   (ii) How were the roads of the mountain?

   (iii) The opposite word of the 'steep' is

   (iv) What is the meaning of the word 'winding'?

   (v) Find two nouns and two adjectives from the lines.

   Nouns ___________ ___________ Adjectives ___________ ___________

Very Short Answer Type Questions

3. Which country did Passepartout belong to?

4. What was the distance between New York and San Fransisco?

Short Answer Type Questions

5. What bet did Mr Fogg lay with his friends?

6. How did the driver manage to pass the broken bridge?

Long Answer Type Question

7. How did Passepartout help in removing the Red Indians from the train?

Language Based Questions

1. Match the following words with their opposites.

	Column A		Column B
(i)	Shrill	(a)	Maximum
(ii)	Minimum	(b)	Quickly
(iii)	Load	(c)	Low
(iv)	Slowly	(d)	Separated
(v)	Joined	(e)	Unload

2. Write two words that rhyme with each of the following.

Rocky _______ _______   Train _______ _______

Track _______ _______   Lost _______ _______

3. The following words are taken from the chapter and are jumbled. Rearrange them to make proper words.

(i) NDSFRIE __________   (ii) NTNULE __________

(iii) RINTA __________   (iv) FICPACI __________

4. Describe in your words your most memorable journey so far.

Malu Bhalu

Text Based Questions

1. State 'T' for true and 'F' for false statements.

(i) Malu was a brave girl.

(ii) Malu did not know how to catch fish.

(iii) Mother asked Malu to wait till summer when she wanted to go out.

(iv) Malu was dumb.

(v) Swimming came naturally to Malu.

2. Read the following lines of the poem and answer the questions that follow.

> High up in an icy lair,
> Lived a little polar bear
> Snow white, snow bright was her mane,
> Malu Bhalu was her name.

(i) What was the name of the Bhalu?

____

(ii) Where did Malu live?

____

(iii) What kind of bear was Malu?

____

(iv) Write the meanings of the following words.

(a) Lair ___________

(b) Mane ___________

Very Short Answer Type Questions

3. Who is the main character of the poem?

4. From which language was this poem translated?

Short Answer Type Questions

5. What is the reason Malu gave to her mother for going out?

6. Why are Malu and her mother called brave?

Language Based Questions

1. Match the following with their opposites.

	Column A		Column B
(i)	Special	(a)	Loose
(ii)	Natural	(b)	Near
(iii)	Patient	(c)	Ordinary
(iv)	Far	(d)	Artificial
(v)	Tight	(e)	Impatient

2. Look at this picture and write a few lines on it.

Chapter 2

Who Will Be Ningthou?

Indira Mukherjee

Text Based Questions

1. State 'T' for true and 'F' for false statements.

   (i) The king had four children.

   (ii) The eldest son was made the future king.

   (iii) Sanatombi was a kind child.

   (iv) The Ningthou stopped thinking about his meeyam.

   (v) Sanatombi was worthy of becoming the king.

2. Read the following lines of the story and answer the questions that follow.
The Ningthou and Leima were watching Sanatombi, their five year old daughter. She looked sad and lonely.

   (i) Why did Sanatombi look sad?

   ____

   (ii) What does Ningthou and Leima mean in English?

     (a) Two nouns   _______________   _______________

     (b) One verb   _______________

     (c) One adjective _______________

     (d) One pronoun _______________

   (iii) Find the following from the lines.

   ____

Very Short Answer Type Question

3. Who is the author of this story?

____

Short Answer Type Questions

5. How did Ningthou want to select the future king?

6. What did Sanajaoba do in the contest?

Long Answer Type Questions

8. Why were Ningthou and Leima loved by their meeyam?

9. Draw a character sketch of Sanatombi.

Language Based Questions

1. Find the words from the chapter that mean the following.

    (i) A four letter word that means 'quiet'.

    (ii) To strike or bite something with its boak.

    (iii) Stretch out one's body or neck in order to see something.

2. Make sentences from the following words.

    (i) Mount

    (ii) Relief

    (iii) Soul

3. Describe any contest that you have participated in. How did you feel being a contestant?

4. List any four things that you can do to save our environment.

    (i)

    (ii)

    (iii)

    (iv)

[Chapter **1**]

Articles

1. Fill in the blanks by using articles ('a', 'an' and 'the').

(i) ___________ apple a day keeps the doctor away.

(ii) Raj Kapoor was ___________ entertainer.

(iii) ___________ Taj Mahal is in Agra.

(iv) Komal is ___________ good girl.

(v) We had two sandwiches and ___________ cake.

2. Complete the paragraph by using articles.

We went into (i)______ forest. (ii)______ forest was dense and full of wild animals. I took (iii)______ umbrella and (iv)______ water bottle with me. We also had (v)______ tent so that we could lay it and sleep at night. (vi)______ elephant passed by and we spotted (vii)______ hyena and (viii)______ deer too. My friend got afraid when (ix)______ sun set down. Luckily, I had got (x)______ torch. I lighted it so that my friend does not get frightened.

3. Underline the article which is used incorrectly in the following sentences.

(i) A Himalayas are located in Nepal and India.

(ii) I had an mango shake for brunch.

(iii) He saw a ostrich at the zoo.

(iv) An President of India lives in Rashtrapati Bhawan.

(v) He is a Prime Minister of India.

4. Put smiley ☺ in front of sentences with correct articles and frowney ☹ in front of incorrect.

(i) We all had a ice-cream. ○

(ii) The United States is a rich country. ○

(iii) Rashi went to see an doctor. ○

(iv) Kashish ate a pizza for lunch. ○

(v) This is an pair of shoes. ○

Nouns and Pronouns

1. Separate the Common Nouns and Proper Nouns from the list below.

> *Car, Rohan, President, Soldier, Google, Maruti, Doctor, Dr Sunanda, Toothpaste, Closeup, Dog, Father-in-law, Police Station, Vasant Kunj, Capital, Bunty, Niece, Cadbury, Chocolate, Esselworld*

Common Noun	Proper Noun

2. Fill in the appropriate collective nouns from the box .

> board   album   cloud   regiment   crew
> pack   army   wad   litter   bunch

(i) A ___________ of dust.

(ii) An ___________ of stamps.

(iii) A ___________ of keys.

(iv) A ___________ of cards.

(v) A ___________ of directors.

(vi) A ___________ of soldiers.

(vii) An ___________ of ants.

(viii) A ___________ of sailors.

(ix) A ___________ of kittens.

(x) A ___________ of notes.

3. Fill in the blanks.

(i) Fox   Foxes   (ii) Puppy _______________

(iii) Thief _______________   (iv) _______________ Judges

(v) Cow _______________   (vi) Calf _______________

(vii) _______________ Chocolates   (viii) City _______________

(ix) _______________ Towns   (x) Country _______________

4. Write the missing gender in the following.

(i) Uncle _______________   (ii) King _______________

(iii) _______________ Governess   (iv) _______________ Daughter-in-law

(v) Nephew _______________   (vi) Host _______________

(vii) _______________ Madam   (viii) Shepherd _______________

(ix) Waiter _______________   (x) _______________ Heroine

(xi) Widower _______________   (xii) Earl _______________

5. Tick (✓) the correct option.

(i) Which of the following is not an abstract noun?

(a) Goodness ☐   (b) Bravery ☐

(c) Family ☐   (d) Childhood ☐

(ii) Family is a _______________ noun.

(a) Common ☐   (b) Proper ☐

(c) Abstract ☐   (d) Collective ☐

(iii) Which of the following is a collective noun?

(a) Team ☐   (b) Books ☐

(c) Marbles ☐   (d) Ships ☐

(iv) Which of the following is a common noun?

(a) London ☐   (b) Delhi ☐

(c) America ☐   (d) Birds ☐

(v) I saw a <u>bunch</u> of grapes. What type of noun is the underlined word?

(a) Common Noun ☐   (b) Proper Noun ☐

(c) Collective Noun ☐   (d) Pronoun ☐

Chapter 3

Conjunctions

1. Underline the conjunctions used in the following sentences.

    (i) He is poor but honest.

    (ii) He sells mangoes and oranges.

    (iii) We will not play the match if it rains.

    (iv) Rakshit went to Paris and had a great time.

    (v) Sam likes Ron because he is always cheerful.

2. Join the following sentences using conjunctions.

    (i) (a) Radha is dancing.

    (b) Rashmi is skipping.

    ____

    (ii) (a) Ice is cold.

    (b) Fire is hot.

    ____

    (iii) (a) Sujay went to the bank.

    (b) Sakshi went to the bank.

    ____

    (iv) (a) Akash goes to school.

    (b) Aradhya stays at home.

    ____

    (v) (a) Rama is poor.

    (b) Rama is honest.

    ____

3. Use the words in the box to fill in the blanks.

while	when	as	because	since	for

   (i) She stole the money _________________ her brother needed to pay the school fees.

  (ii) _________________ we were in New Zealand, we visited many orchards.

 (iii) _________________ I am on leave tomorrow, there will be no English lesson.

 (iv) He came dripping wet _________________ it was raining heavily at school.

  (v) _________________ I was passing his house, I heard a loud scream.

 (vi) Shivam waited _________________ Rohan poured a cup of tea.

4. Some of the sentences mentioned below have incorrect conjunctions used in them. Identify them and rewrite them properly.

   (i) Rajiv is poor and honest.

  ____

  (ii) Ram and Shyam went to the church.

  ____

 (iii) We waited and the train arrived.

  ____

 (iv) He failed and he worked hard.

  ____

  (v) Harry is a good and kind boy.

  ____

5. Fill in the blanks using suitable conjunctions.

   (i) Wait here _________________ I return.

  (ii) We must eat _________________ die.

 (iii) Tom goes to school _________________ his sister stays in a creche.

 (iv) Anne is tall _________________ Mary is taller.

  (v) I shall buy it _________________ I have money.

 (vi) Run fast _________________ you will miss the train.

Chapter 4

Adjectives

1. Underline the adjectives in the following sentences.

   (i)   The left-handed man had a boyish face.

   (ii) I need a soft and silky yarn to make her dress.

   (iii) Dhoni is the best captain.

   (iv) The blue, swift cat leaped over the wooden, rotten fence before the angry dog could reach it.

   (v)   He stared at the young lady.

2. Read the paragraph and underline the adjectives in it.

   The quick brown fox jumped over the lazy dog. I was sleeping in the drawing room when this happened. My old friend who was staying with me told me about this. The angry dog bit the fox but the fox ran away.

3. Complete the table by filling in the blanks.

S No	Positive Degree	Comparative Degree	Superlative Degree
(i)	Fast	__________	__________
(ii)	__________	Closer	__________
(iii)	__________	__________	Best
(iv)	Much	__________	__________
(v)	__________	Thinner	__________
(vi)	Lengthy	__________	__________
(vii)	Careful	__________	__________
(viii)	__________	__________	Brightest
(ix)	__________	More polite	__________
(x)	__________	Busier	__________

Prepositions

1. Fill in the blanks by choosing the correct option from the choices.

  (i) The car ran _________________ the dog.

     (a) onto   ☐   (b) into   ☐

     (c) over   ☐   (d) in   ☐

  (ii) I live _______________ New Delhi.

     (a) on   ☐   (b) in   ☐

     (c) upon   ☐   (d) onto   ☐

  (iii) The shop is located _______________ the main road.

     (a) in   ☐   (b) upon   ☐

     (c) on   ☐   (d) into   ☐

  (iv) The train passed _______________ the tunnel.

     (a) on   ☐   (b) upon   ☐

     (c) into   ☐   (d) through   ☐

  (v) He died _______________ typhoid.

     (a) at   ☐   (b) in   ☐

     (c) of   ☐   (d) into   ☐

2. In the following sentences the prepositions have been used incorrectly. Spot the error and write the correct word in the space provided.

	Incorrect	Correct
(i) He jumped on the river.	__________	__________
(ii) Rashi has not yet recovered with her illness.	__________	__________
(iii) Do not cry onto spilt milk.	__________	__________
(iv) Be careful of what you say.	__________	__________
(v) We went on the shop.	__________	__________

4. Circle the correct preposition in the following sentences.

   (i) Shyam ran (across, into) the street.   (ii) Let us sit (in, under) a shady tree.

 (iii) The cat jumped (in, on) the sofa.   (iv) We talked (about, on) many things.

  (v) Do not quarrel (on, with) me.   (vi) Beware (on,of) pickpockets.

 (vii) He was born (of, on) rich parents.   (viii) We should not laugh (at, over) beggars.

 (ix) Fill the bottle (into, with) cold water.   (x) She prays (to, at) God daily.

5. Make sentences using the following prepositions.

   (i) Across ____

  (ii) Through ____

 (iii) Under ____

 (iv) Onto ____

  (v) By ____

6. Look at the picture and complete the sentences with the help of prepositions.

   (i) _______________ this picture, I can see a family _______________ the kitchen.

  (ii) There is a dish full of fruits _______________ the table.

 (iii) The mother is holding a vase _______________ her hand.

 (iv) The son and daughter are sitting _______________ the table smiling _______________ each other.

  (v) There are beautiful cupboards _______________ the wall.

Tenses

1. Identify the tense of the following sentences.

   (i) I am a good boy.

   (ii) He will go there at 4 pm.

   (iii) Nikita was afraid of dark when she was small.

   (iv) The sun rises in the East.

   (v) Pallavi is not well today.

2. Fill in the blanks by using the correct form of tenses of the words given in the box.

> do   rain   display   play   go

   (i) The notice was _______________ on the board.

   (ii) It was _______________ when we left home.

   (iii) I went to _______________ in the evening.

   (iv) Navin _______________ there tomorrow.

   (v) Let us _______________ it again.

3. Convert the following sentences into past tense.

   (i) I am doing this.

   (ii) They are playing there.

   (iii) Ram is at the zoo.

   (iv) Tanuj plays the guitar.

   (v) Rashmi will visit her parents.

4. Convert the following sentences into future tense.

   (i) I play in the park.

   (ii) He is coming to my home.

  (iii) I splashed water on my face.

  (iv) Rahul played in the park.

   (v) Navneet is riding a cycle.

5. The following sentences are jumbled. Rearrange them to make them meaningful. Also identify their tense.

   (i) sold/Hitesh/bike/Quikr/on/his

   (ii) amazing/was/Abdul Kalam/an/person

  (iii) him/I/Metro/station/met/at/the

  (iv) am/reading/book/the/now/I

   (v) will/there/tomorrow/go/we/meet/him/to

  (vi) you/take/chair/please/can/this/?

6. Listed below are the past form of a few words. Write down the present form of these words in the space given.

(i) Stole	_________	(ii) Bought	_________
(iii) Ate	_________	(iv) Blew	_________
(v) Bit	_________	(vi) Flopped	_________
(vii) Chided	_________	(viii) Hid	_________

Chapter 7

Verbs

1. Underline the verbs in the following sentences.

   (i) He stole the book.   (ii) I met him yesterday.

  (iii) They cooked a delicious meal.   (iv) Raman saw a rainbow.

   (v) I watered and pruned the plants.

2. In some of the following sentences, there is a mistake associated with verbs. Identify those incorrect sentences. Tick (✓) against correct and cross (×) against incorrect one.

   (i) I is a good man.   (ii) He is good for nothing.

  (iii) Rajat and Shashi am friends.   (iv) Golu meet with an accident.

   (v) Teepu has a good day today.   (vi) We going to support the country.

  (vii) They are playing cricket now.   (viii) She will go there tomorrow.

  (ix) They is too good.   (x) I myself did it.

3. Use helping verbs to complete the following sentences.

> *should, may, could, can, may*

   (i) I ____________ do this.

   (ii) ____________ I use the washroom?

  (iii) He ____________ play the guitar when he was four.

  (iv) Everybody ____________ go there once in a lifetime.

   (v) It ____________ rain today.

4. Use the correct form of the verb given in the bracket to complete the sentences.

   (i) I ____________ him an apple. (*give*)

   (ii) The thief was ____________ red handed. (*catch*)

  (iii) The sun ____________ in the East. (*rise*)

  (iv) He ____________ there yesterday. (*go*)

   (v) Rajat ____________ there daily. (*go*)

Chapter 8

Adverbs

1. Underline the adverbs in the following sentences.

    (i) Ravi came quickly.   (ii) Sonam is very beautiful.

    (iii) Saksham is quite strong.   (iv) She seldom came here.

    (v) We often talk to ourselves.   (vi) The doctor is coming immediately.

    (vii) The boys ran forward.   (viii) I went there twice.

    (ix) The glass is nearly full.   (x) How are you today?

    (xi) She painted the room slowly and beautifully.

2. Fill in the blanks using the adverbs given in the box.

> *once, very, outside, bravely, entirely, why*

    (i) Rohan is waiting __________.   (ii) I have met him __________ in my life.

    (iii) The soldiers fought __________.   (iv) __________ are you so late?

    (v) Kiran was __________ angry.   (vi) The room is __________ full.

3. Rewrite the following sentences using the adverbs mentioned in the brackets.

    (i) He hasn't reached. (yet)   (ii) Kanishka is late for work. (always)

    (iii) I ran to save her life. (quickly)   (iv) Shweta is fair. (extremely)

    (v) Ram punched him. (thrice)   (vi) She prayed to God. (silently)

    (vii) He visits his parents. (rarely)

4. Fill in the blanks by using the correct option given in the brackets.

    (i) He is always in a rush. I don't understand why he walks so __________ .(quick/quickly)

    (ii) I prefer studying in the library. It's always __________ .(quietly/quiet)

    (iii) Megha __________ (happy/happily) took the assistant job.

    (iv) Sonakshi dances __________ (beautifully/beautiful). She has been taking classes since she was 5 years old.

    (v) They speak French very __________(good/well). They lived in France for two years.

    (vi) My neighbour always plays __________ (loud/loudly) music on the weekends.

Chapter 9

Sentences

1. Divide each of the following sentences into Subject and Predicate.

(i) Raman went into the class.

Subject _______________________ Predicate _______________________

(ii) He is a clever and dishonest man.

Subject _______________________ Predicate _______________________

(iii) You come at once.

Subject _______________________ Predicate _______________________

(iv) We came together.

Subject _______________________ Predicate _______________________

(v) The Himalayas are located in Northern India.

Subject _______________________ Predicate _______________________

(vi) The poor guy went home without food.

Subject _______________________ Predicate _______________________

2. Match the subject in Column I with the predicate in Column II.

Column I	Column II
(i) I	(a) is a crazy girl.
(ii) Rahat	(b) am going to school.
(iii) The doctor	(c) are friends.
(iv) Komal and Satya	(d) went to his clinic.
(v) She	(e) is a good person.

3. Identify the type of sentence from the following (Imperative, Exclamatory, Declarative or Interrogative).

   (i) Give me that phone. ___________________

   (ii) Alas! India has lost the semi-final. ___________________

   (iii) The Sun sets in the West. ___________________

   (iv) Where is your I-card? ___________________

   (v) Hurrah! We have won the match. ___________________

4. Convert the following sentences into interrogative sentences.

   (i) Someone stole my jacket.

____

   (ii) Simran's coat is of red colour.

____

   (iii) We kept the notebook on the table.

____

   (iv) I went to the market.

____

   (v) Five people went to the party.

____

5. There is something wrong with these sentences. Write them correctly.

   (i) Sunita has been in the hospital since 10 o clock.

____

   (ii) Sunday is The first Day of the week.

____

   (iii) navin Sheetal and I went to the hotel.

____

   (iv) we came here last night.

____

   (v) May I have that pen.

____

Letter Writing

Write a letter to your friend requesting him/her to celebrate Diwali with you.

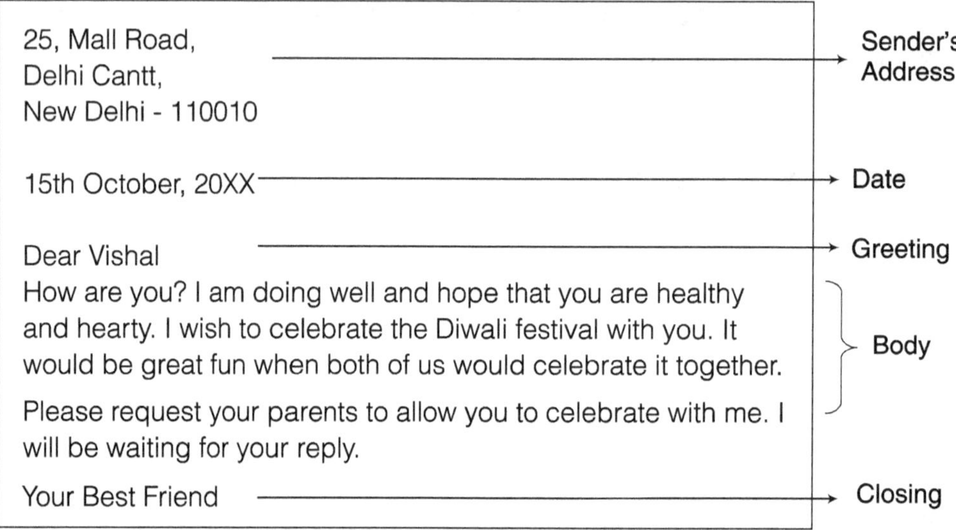

1. You have been invited by your friend on his birthday party. He lives in a different city. You are unable to attend the party as you have an exam on the next day of the birthday party. The following letter has been written by you expressing thanks to him for inviting you for the party. Complete the missing parts in the letter.

Janakpuri,
New Delhi-58

17th August, 20XX

Dear Roshan
Thank you for inviting me to your birthday party.

____

____

____

Yours affectionately
Samir

2. Write a letter to Santa Claus requesting him to give you a gift on Christmas. A few hints for the letter are given below :

- Describe the gift.
- How would you use the gift?
- Mention why you need that gift.

3. You are the Monitor of your class. Write a letter to the Monitor of a different section inviting him to play a friendly cricket match with your class. A few hints for the letter are given below :

- Cricket match of 10 overs
- The PT Teacher will be the Umpire
- To be played in lunch time
- List of players to be given beforehand

4. Write a letter to your favourite teacher wishing her Happy Teachers' Day. Also, thank her for the guidance given to you. You are Rakshit of Class 5th 'A'.

5. Write a letter to your cousin inviting him to attend your birthday party. It should not exceed 80 words.

Chapter 2

Paragraph Writing

Write a paragraph on the topic 'Your Hobby'.

> My hobby is gardening. Whenever I get time, I like to spend it in my garden. I go to a nursery and purchase saplings of seasonal flowers. Then I plant them in my garden. I also like to prune my plants, add manure to them on a regular basis and water them regularly. It gives me great joy when I see my plants flower. I have got different varieties of flowering and decorative plants and keep adding to them from time to time. Gardening is indeed one of the best hobbies as it allows one to spend time with mother nature.

1. Write a paragraph on the cleanliness drive organised by your school. Keep the following points in mind while writing it.

   - When was the drive held?
   - Who inaugurated the drive?
   - Who all participated in the drive?
   - What activities were performed in the drive?

2. Write a paragraph on the topic "My first day in school."
   The following points can be used to write the paragraph

   - Who dropped you at school?
   - How did you feel?
   - Did you make any friends?
   - How was your class teacher?

3. Write a paragraph on your favourite personality.

The following points can be used to write the paragraph.

- Why is he/she your favourite?
- What qualities do you like in him/her?

4. Write a paragraph on the Holi Festival.

You may use the following hints

- When and why is it celebrated?
- How is it celebrated?
- Festival of colours

5. Write a paragraph on "Save Water". You may use the following hints

- Use a tumbler for saving or to water plants instead of a hose.
- Repair leaking taps.
- Use a bucket for taking bath instead of using the shower.

6. Write a paragraph on 'My best friend'.

Chapter 3

Notice Writing

You are the Principal of ABC Public School. Your school is organising a picnic for the students of class 5th. Write a notice to inform the students.

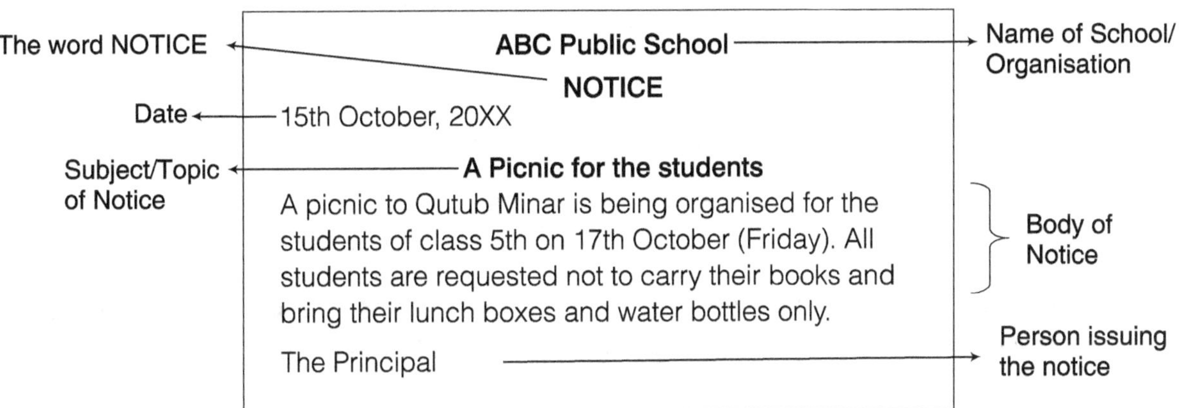

1. The following notice is given below. Read it and answer the questions that follow:

> **Delhi Public School**
> **NOTICE**
> 15th October, 20XX
>
> **Annual Day Function**
> The Annual Day of our school will be held on 20th November, 20XX in school auditorium. The students who are interested to take part may give their names to Mrs Pant.
> Cultural Incharge

(i) Which day is announced in the notice?

(ii) To whom were the interested students to give their names?

(iii) When is the Annual Day going to be celebrated?

(iv) Who has issued the notice?

2. The titles and sentences in the following notice are jumbled up. Rearrange them and rewrite the notice to make it meaningful.

<table>
<tr><td>Donate Generously</td><td>1st August, 20xx</td></tr>
<tr><td colspan="2">All students who are willing to donate can bring the clothes alongwith a letter of permission from their parents. Our school is organising a camp for donating old clothes for the Nepal Earthquake Victims. The last date for donation is 20th August.   NOTICE

Jeet Public School</td></tr>
</table>

3. The below mentioned notice is made by Rinku. He has made some mistakes while writing the notice. Identify the mistakes and rewrite the notice correctly.

<table>
<tr><td colspan="2" align="center">Notice</td></tr>
<tr><td colspan="2" align="center">Independence Day Holiday</td></tr>
<tr><td colspan="2" align="center">K.D. Public School</td></tr>
<tr><td colspan="2">The school was closed on 15th August on the occasion of Independence Day.</td></tr>
<tr><td>It is reopen on the 17th August (Monday).</td><td>The Headmistress</td></tr>
</table>

4. The notice given below is about the change in the timings of a children's club in your neighbourhood. The new timings are from 6 PM to 8 PM.

Complete the following notice by filling up the blank spaces.

NOTICE

Blooming Buds has got new timings with the advent of Monsoons. The club

____

____

____

Club Incharge

5. You are the Monitor of your class. Your class is going to play a friendly football match with class V-'C' on 18th August.

The match would be held on the ground number 1 during lunch time. Write a notice for the non-participating students of your class to be a part of audience and cheer your team.

6. The flag-hoisting ceremony will be held in your society at 8 AM on the occasion of Independence Day.

Write a notice inviting all the children between 6 to 10 years to be a part of it. They must come in ethnic wear and should reach the main ground by 7:45 AM.

Chapter 4

Diary Writing

Write a diary entry of your birthday.

21st September, 20XX —————————————————→ Date

Today was my birthday. I have turned 10 today. My parents
were the first one to wish me a happy birthday! I went to school
and distributed sweets among my classmates and my teacher.
Everyone sang 'Happy Birthday' and clapped for me! I felt so
special! My parents had organised a party in the evening at my
home. All my friends from my neighbourhood came to the party.
I cut the cake and took the blessings of my parents. Everyone
gave me gifts and I thanked them for coming to my party. I
enjoyed the day very much!

Body

1. Write a diary entry expressing your best day ever in life.

2. You have found a cave inside a tree with your elder brother. Write your experience in the form of a diary entry.

3. Write a diary entry about how you spent the last day in school before the summer break.

4. Try to recall any dream that you dreamt at night. Write about it in the diary entry space given below.

5. Write a diary entry about all your fears and things that scare you.

Chapter 5

Report Writing

You have recently visited a village. Write a report about your visit.

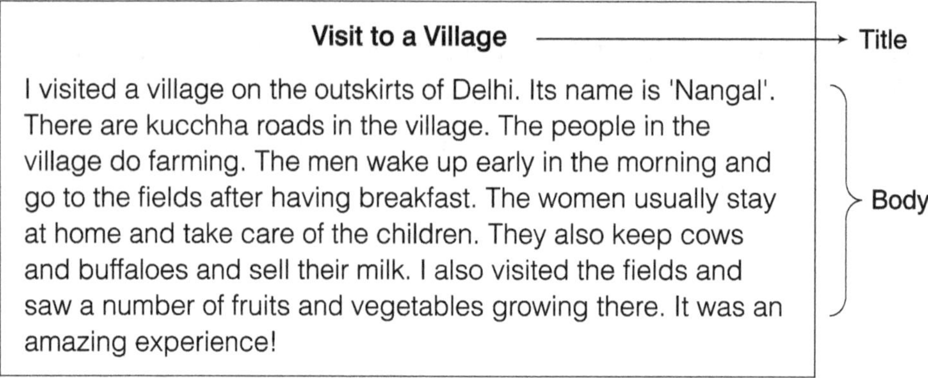

1. The following report has few errors in it. Identify the errors and rewrite the report properly.
Also give a suitable title to it.

Our class go to see the Republic Day Parade. We assemble at our school at 6 AM. Our
class teacher counted the number of students present. We board the bus and got down
on the venue. The parade is very interesting. We enjoy a lot. I liked the air-show the
most. I hope that I get a chance to see it again.

2. Write a report on a visit to a museum. You may use the following clues

- Start with a short introduction
- List the things that you saw in the museum
- Mention the 3 things that you liked the most

3. Write a report on any match that you have enjoyed watching. You may use the following clues to create the report.

- Type of match
- How did you watch it? (In stadium or on TV etc)
- Why did you find it interesting?
- Which team did you support?
- Who won the match?

4. You recently celebrated the Independence Day by flying kites. Write a report on it using the clues given below.

- Introduction—Mention that people celebrate the day in North India by flying kites of different colours and sizes.
- Describe the weather on that day.
- With whom did you fly kites?
- How many kites were there in the sky? (approximately)
- How was the atmosphere?
- Finally write about the most common kite that was being flown? (The tricoloured kite etc)

Chapter 6

Story Writing

Write a story with the title 'The Fox without a Tail'.

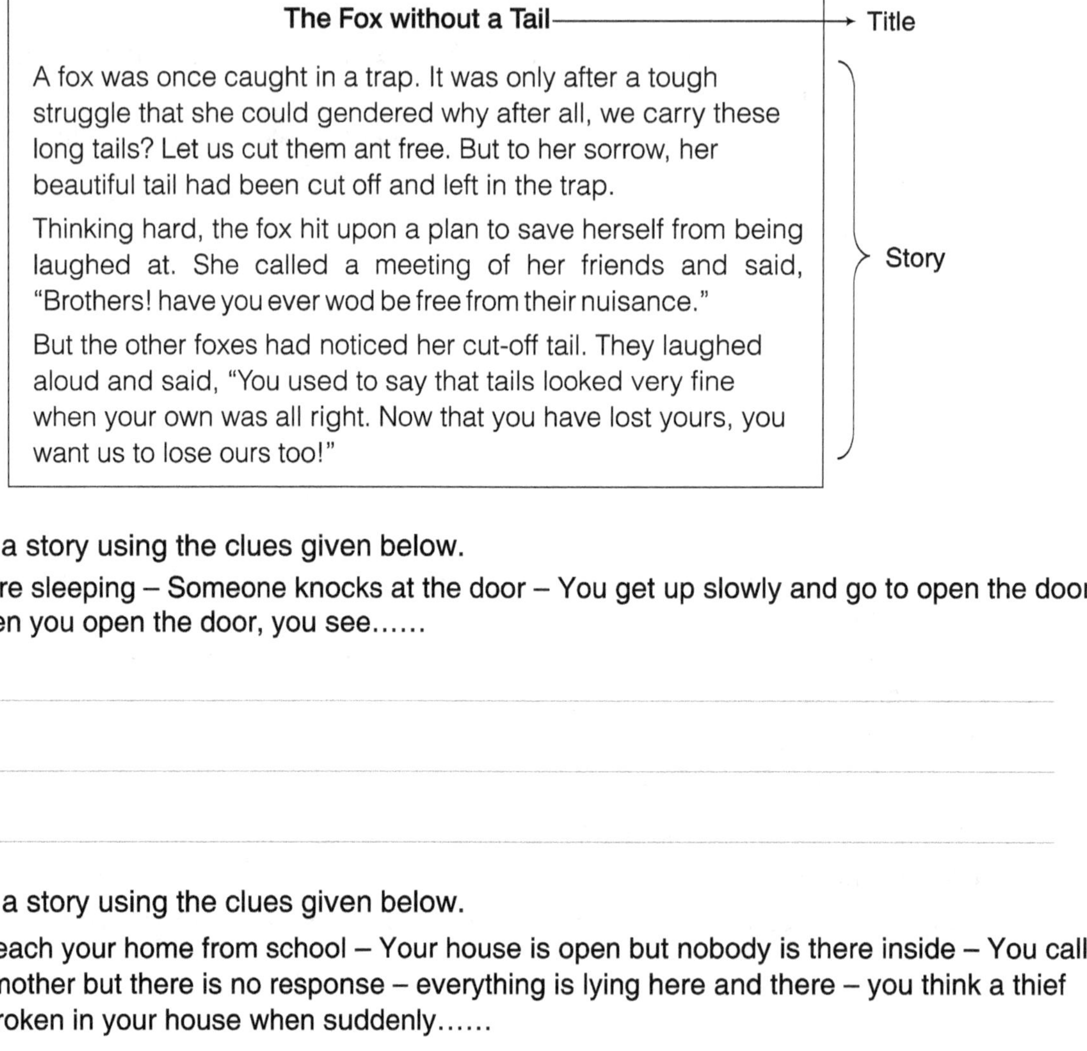

1. Write a story using the clues given below.

You are sleeping – Someone knocks at the door – You get up slowly and go to open the door – When you open the door, you see……

2. Write a story using the clues given below.

You reach your home from school – Your house is open but nobody is there inside – You call your mother but there is no response – everything is lying here and there – you think a thief has broken in your house when suddenly……

3. A story is jumbled up below. Rearrange and rewrite it in the proper sequence.

1. A mouse was running up and down upon the lion.
2. Once a lion was asleep in his den.
3. The lion got up and placed his paw upon the little mouse.
4. The mouse thanked the lion.
5. The mouse asked for forgiveness and said that one day he would help the lion.
6. The lion forgave him and let him go.
7. One day the lion was caught in a net by the hunters.
8. The mouse saw that the lion needed his help.
9. The hunters had gone out for a break.
10. The mouse cut the net and set the lion free.
11. In this way, the mouse kept his promise.
12. The lion thanked him a lot for saving his life.

4. Write a story using the clues given below.

A little boy came running excitedly to his mother.... He said that there is someone in the woods who is mocking at him... It repeats whatever he says ......

5. Write a story which conveys the message "God helps those who help themselves".

Chapter 7

Picture Comprehension

Sample 1   Look at the picture given below and answer the questions that follow.

(i)   What is the boy doing?

Ans. The boy is standing on the weighing machine.

(ii)   What is the girl doing?

Ans. The girl is looking at the boy.

(iii)   What else do you see in the picture?

Ans. I see a Teddy Bear that is lying on the floor.

Sample 2   Look at the picture given below and write a few lines on it.

A birthday party is going on. A girl who has turned 4 years old is celebrating her birthday. There is one more girl and two boys in the party. The cake is kept on the table and the girl's mother is bringing ice-creams for the kids.

A few of the kids are wearing caps. The pet dog (puppy) of the girl is also attending the party. The birthday girl is about to blow the candles.

1. Go through the picture and answer the questions that follow.

   (i) What is the giant doing?

  (ii) What is the other man doing?

 (iii) What kind of mood does the giant seem to be in?

2. Look at the picture given below and write a paragraph on it. Suggest a suitable title also.

3. Look at the picture given below and answer the following questions:

(i) Where is the child?

____

(ii) What is the child doing?

____

(iii) What is the child's mother doing?

____

4. Look at the picture below and write down a few lines on it. Also give a suitable title to it.

____

____

____

5. Look at the picture below and answer the following questions.

(i) What do you see in the picture?

____

(ii) Why is the cat running after the mouse?

____

(iii) Would she be able to catch the mouse?

____

6. Look at the picture below and write a few lines on it. Also suggest a suitable title for it.

____

____

____

____

Worksheet 1

1. *Read the passage and answer the questions that follow.*

In the rapid rat race for development we have forgotten that it is our duty to give back to the nature twice as much as we take. A single tree fulfils so many of our needs but how many of us realise that one fine day when this resource of trees finish their selfless service to us, we will be left empty handed staring into a blank future.

Progress is very much needed for the evolution of mankind but what we need to look into is the pace of this progress. Being fast is indeed a necessity to keep yourself abreast with changing times but fighting a major issue like Global Warming by taking small steps like planting trees and raising awareness is also equally important.

Come forward, Let's plant trees together …!!!

Questions

I. Choose the correct option.

(i) It is our duty to give back to the nature

(a) thrice as much as we take ☐ (b) as much as we take ☐

(c) twice as much as we take ☐ (d) half as much as we take ☐

(ii) The race for development is a

(a) fox race ☐ (b) rat race ☐

(c) bee race ☐ (d) dog race ☐

(iii) We should take ____________ steps to protect nature.

(a) small ☐ (b) baby ☐

(c) long ☐ (d) no ☐

II. Answer the following questions.

(i) Which issue is mentioned in the passage?

____

(ii) What have we forgotten in the rat race for development?

____

(iii) What does the passage urge us to do?

____

III. Do as directed.

    (i) The antonym of 'forward' is _________________________ .

    (ii) The antonym of 'major' is _________________________ .

2. *Read the poem and answer the questions that follow.*

A Friend From Above

I prayed for you before we met …
Not knowing what you'd be,
I asked the Lord to send a friend.
One chosen just for me…
I asked that they'd be Godly
With wisdom of his ways.
A friend to help and guide me
In the troubles of these days…
So often in life, we need someone
To listen while we talk.

Someone who will not condemn or judge
But encourage us as we walk.
The narrow road we choose to follow
May sometimes make us stumble.
But to have a friend to catch our fall
Teaches us to be humble.
When I asked The Lord to send a friend
Though many came and went…
He gave much more than I asked
For you are the friend he sent.

—By Anonymous

Questions

I. Choose the correct option.

The poet wanted a friend to

    (a) guide him   ☐   (b) hide him   ☐

    (c) misguide him   ☐   (d) trouble him   ☐

II. Answer the following questions.

    (i) What did the poet pray for?

    (ii) Describe the kind of friend the poet wants.

    (iii) What happened when the poet asked for a friend?

III. Write two rhyming words of the following words.

    (i) Met _________ _________   (ii) Catch _________ _________

    (iii) Stumble _________ _________   (iv) May _________ _________

Worksheet 2

1. *Read the passage and answer the questions that follow.*

On 2nd October 2014, Swachh Bharat Mission was launched throughout the length and breadth of the country as a national movement. While leading the mass movement for cleanliness, the Prime Minister encouraged people to fulfil Mahatma Gandhi's dream of a clean and hygienic India.

Shri Narendra Modi himself initiated the cleanliness drive at Mandir Marg Police Station. Picking up the broom to clean the dirt, making Swachh Bharat Abhiyan a mass movement across the nation, the Prime Minister said people should neither litter, nor let others litter. He gave the mantra of '*Na gandagi karenge, Na karne denge*'.

Shri Narendra Modi also invited nine people to join the cleanliness drive and requested each of them to draw nine more into the initiative. By inviting people to participate in the drive, the Swachh Bharat Abhiyan has turned into a national movement. A sense of responsibility has been evoked among the people through the Clean India Movement. With citizens now becoming active participants in cleanliness activities across the nation, the dream of a 'Clean India' once seen by Mahatma Gandhi has begun to get a shape.

Questions

I. Choose the correct option.

   (i) The Swachh Bharat Mission was launched throughout the

      (a) length of the country   (b) breadth of the country

      (c) length and breadth of the country   (d) height of the country

  (ii) The mantra of Swachh Bharat Mission is

      (a) *Gandagi karenge or karne denge*

      (b) *Gandagi karenge par karne nahin denge*

      (c) *Gandagi nahi karenge par karne denge*

      (d) *Na gandagi karenge, na karne denge*

 (iii) The citizens are becoming __________ participants in the mission.

      (a) active   (b) passive

      (c) inactive   (d) None of these

II. Answer the following questions.

   (i) What did Mahatma Gandhi dream of?

(ii) When was 'Swachh Bharat Abhiyan' launched?

____

(iii) How will 'Clean India' become a mass movement?

____

III. Do as directed.

    (i) Find a word from the passage that is the synonym of 'urged'. _____________

    (ii) A word from the passage that means 'throw waste or garbage' is _____________ .

    (iii) The antonym of 'passive' is _____________ .

2. *Read the poem and answer the questions that follow.*

Wild Orange

I walked along the path and there
a flash of eyes, a golden pair,
the pupils slit and feline shy
the creature looked me in the eye.
His colour was an orange shock
a furry, puffed up, fancy frock,
with streaks and lines of creamy hair
he did not break his intense stare.

Frozen bodies, eyes still locked
he seemed no longer to be shocked,
instead now sure I posed no threat
I saw this cat was no one's pet.
There was no collar on his neck,
a wild hunter on a trek,
distracted by some human man,
then off into the grass he ran.

—by Robert Patinson

Questions

  I. Choose the correct option.

    (i) The cat's colour was

      (a) red ☐   (b) purple ☐   (c) green ☐   (d) orange ☐

    (ii) The poet spotted the cat

      (a) in a jungle ☐   (b) in a train ☐   (c) on a road ☐   (d) in his house ☐

  II. Answer the following questions.

    (i) Which animal is described in the poem?

____

    (ii) How did the poet know that the cat was no one's pet?

____

  III. Do as directed.

    (i) Find a word from the poem that means 'relating to or affecting cats or other members of the cat family'. _____________

    (ii) Find a word from the poem that is 'a part of the eye'. _____________

Worksheet 3

1. *Read the passage and answer the questions that follow.*

Walt Disney was born on 5th December, 1901. Disney became one of the best known motion picture producers in the world. He is particularly noted for being a film producer and a popular showman, as well as an innovator in animation and theme park design. Disney is famous for his contributions in the field of entertainment during the 20th century. His first success was through the series, Oswald the Lucky Rabbit which was created by the Disney studio for Charles Mintz of Universal studios.

When Disney asked for a larger budget for his popular Oswald series, Mintz refused and Disney had to quit. Later, Disney and his brother Roy O Disney started from scratch and co-founded Walt Disney productions, now-known as 'The Walt Disney Company'. Today, this company has annual revenues of approximately U.S $35 billion. This success is largely due to a number of the world's most famous fictional characters he and his staff created including Mickey Mouse, a character for which Disney himself was the original voice.

Questions

I. Choose the correct option.

(i) Walt Disney was born on

(a) 5th December, 1902   (b) 5th December, 1903

(c) 5th December, 1901   (d) 5th December, 1910

(ii) The Walt Disney Company has annual revenue of

(a) $35 million   (b) $25 million

(c) $35 billion   (c) $25 billion

(iii) The first success of Walt Disney was through the series

(a) Mickey Mouse   (b) Oswald the Lucky Rabbit

(c) Donald Duck   (d) Tin Tin

II. Answer the following questions.

(i) What is Walt Disney known for?

____

(ii) Which company was founded by Walt Disney?

____

(iii) Name one character created by Walt.

____

III. Write the opposites of the following words.

    (i) Fictional ______________   (ii) Success ______________

IV. Unscramble the following words to create meaningful words from the passage.

    (i) E Y I D S N ______________   (ii) A L N U N A ______________

2. *Read the poem and answer the questions that follow.*

Dirty Face

Where did you get such a dirty face,
My darling dirty-faced child?
I got it from crawling along in the dirt
And biting two buttons of Jeremy's shirt.
I got it from chewing the roots of a rose
And digging for clams in the yard with my nose.
I got it from peeking into a dark cave
And painting myself like a Navajo brave.
I got it from playing with coal in the bin
And signing my name in cement with my chin.
I got if from rolling around on the rug
And giving the horrible dog a big hug.
I got it from finding a lost silver mine
And eating sweet blackberries right off the vine.
I got it from ice-cream and wrestling and tears
And from having more fun than you've had in years.

Questions

I. Answer the following questions.

    (i) Write any four reasons given by the boy for having a dirty face.

____

    (ii) Whose buttons did the boy bite off?

____

    (iii) How did the boy sign his name?

____

II. Find the following from the poem.

    (i) Three Adjectives   ____________   ____________   ____________

    (ii) One Proper Noun   ____________

    (iii) Three Verbs   ____________   ____________   ____________

III. Write the opposites of the following.

    (i) Lost ____________   (ii) Dirty ____________   (iii) Sweet ____________

IV. Write down the meanings of the following words.

    (i) Vine ____________   (ii) Peek ____________   (iii) Clams ____________

Answers

[Literature]

Unit 1

Chapter 1　Ice-Cream Man

Text Based Questions

1. (i) F　　　　(ii) T　　　　(iii) F　　　　**2.** (iii) (c)

Language Based Questions

1. (i) (b)　　　(ii) (c)　　　(iii) (d)　　　(iv) (a)

Chapter 2　Wonderful Waste!

Text Based Questions

1. (i) F　　　　(ii) T　　　　(iii) F　　　　(iv) T

Language Based Questions

1. (i) (d)　　　(ii) (c)　　　(iii) (b)　　　(iv) (a)

3. (i) Travancore, Kerala, Avial, Feast　　(ii) Surveyed, Cooked, Cleaned
(iii) Tempting, Huge, Long

Bamboo Curry

Text Based Questions

1. (i) F　　　　(ii) T　　　　(iii) F　　　　(iv) T

Language Based Questions

1. (i) (c)　　　(ii) (d)　　　(iii) (a)　　　(iv) (b)

Unit 2

Chapter 1　Teamwork

Text Based Questions

1. (i) T　　　　(ii) T　　　　(iii) F

Language Based Questions

1. (i) (b)　　　(ii) (c)　　　(iii) (d)　　　(iv) (a)

4. (i) HOCKEY　　(ii) GOLF　　(iii) CRICKET　　(iv) LUDO　　　(v) CHESS

Chapter 2　Flying Together

Text Based Questions

1. (i) F　　　　(ii) T　　　　(iii) F　　　　(iv) T

Language Based Questions

1. (i) Adjective : Tall; Opposite : Short   (ii) Adjective : Small; Opposite : Large

(iii) Adjective : Wise; Opposite : Foolish

2. (i) impure   (ii) unloaded   (iii) rewrite

4. (i) goose   (ii) hunter   (iii) mouse (iv) fly   (v) cactus   (vi) half

(vii) life   (viii) fungus

Unit 3

Chapter 1   My Shadow

Text Based Questions

1. (i) F   (ii) T   (iii) F   (iv) T   (v) F

Language Based Questions

1. (i) (b)   (ii) (a)   (iii) (d)   (iv) (c)

Chapter 2   Robinson Crusoe Discovers a Footprint

Text Based Questions

1. (i) F   (ii) T   (iii) T   (iv) F

Language Based Questions

1. (i) (b)   (ii) (c)   (iii) (a)

2. (i) Frightened   (ii) Chased

Unit 4

Chapter 1   Crying

Text Based Questions

1. (i) F   (ii) F   (iii) T   (iv) T

Language Based Questions

1. (i) Open   (ii) Up   (iii) Last   (iv) Happiness   (v) Use

2. (i) SPLASH   (ii) THROW   (iii) PEOPLE   (iv) PILLOW   (v) MUST

5. (i) (d)   (ii) (c)   (iii) (b)   (iv) (a)

Chapter 2   My Elder Brother

Text Based Questions

1. (i) F   (ii) F   (iii) T   (iv) F   (v) T

Language Based Questions

2. (ii) Unimportant   (iii) Unpunctual   (iv) Disobedient   (v) Dishonour

(vi) Unhappy   (vii) Improper

3. (i) (d)   (ii) (c)   (iii) (a)   (iv) (e)   (v) (b)

Unit 5

Chapter 1   The Lazy Frog

Text Based Questions

1. (i) F   (ii) T   (iii) F   (iv) F

Language Based Questions

1. (i) B   (ii) C   (iii) B

2. (i) lazy   (ii) old   (iii) he   (v) open

4. (i) Shoes   (ii) Fear   (iii) Frog

Chapter 2   Rip Van Winkle

Text Based Questions

1. (i) F   (ii) T   (iii) F   (iv) T   (v) F

Language Based Questions

1. (i) WEEDS   (ii) WRINKLES   (iii) DAYDREAM   (iv DESCEND   (v) BARREL

2. (i) VILLAGE   (ii) MARBLES   (iii) ECHOED   (iv) RUBBED

Unit 6

Chapter 1   Class Discussion

Text Based Questions

1. (i) F   (ii) F   (iii) T   (iv) F   (v) F

Language Based Questions

2. (i) (c)   (ii) (d)   (iii) (b)   (iv) (a)

Chapter 2   The Talkative Barber

Text Based Questions

1. (i) F   (ii) T   (iii) F   (iv) T   (v) T

Language Based Questions

1. (i) A   (ii) C   (iii) B   (iv) C   (v) A

Unit 7

Chapter 1   Topsy-Turvy Land

Text Based Questions

1. (i) F   (ii) T   (iii) F   (iv) F   (v) T

Language Based Questions

1. (i) Grand   (ii) Pleasure   (iii) Sea   (iv) Travel

3. (i) Grand   (ii) Street   (iii) Beat   (iv) Thermometer

Chapter 2 Gulliver's Travels

Text Based Questions

1. (i) F   (ii) T   (iii) F   (iv) T   (v) F

Language Based Questions

1. (i) Barren   (ii) Apron   (iii) Explore   (iv) Scream   (v) Spring

3. (i) mild/moderate (ii) fertile   (iii) impossible (iv) gently

Unit 8

Chapter 1 Nobody's Friend

Text Based Questions

1. (i) T   (ii) T   (iii) F   (iv) F   (v) F

Language Based Questions

1. (i) take   (ii) bell   (iii) enemy   (iv) wind

2. (i) FOE   (ii) SWEET   (iii) BICYCLE   (iv) SOMEBODY

    (v) CONFECTIONERY

Chapter 2 The Little Bully

Text Based Questions

1. (i) T   (ii) F   (iii) F   (iv) T   (v) F

Language Based Questions

1. (i) pull   (ii) civilised/quiet (iii) calm/indifferent (iv) polite/soft   (v) complain

3. (i) B   (ii) C   (iii) A   (iv) B

Unit 9

Chapter 1 Sing a Song of People

Text Based Questions

1. (i) T   (ii) T   (iii) T   (iv) F

Language Based Questions

1. (i) (c)   (ii) (d)   (iii) (b)   (iv) (e)   (v) (a)

Chapter 2 Around the World

Text Based Questions

1. (i) F   (ii) T   (iii) F   (iv) T   (v) F

Language Based Questions

1. (i) (c)   (ii) (a)   (iii) (e)   (iv) (b)   (v) (d)

3. (i) FRIENDS   (ii) TUNNEL   (iii) TRAIN   (iv) PACIFIC

Chapter 1   Malu Bhalu

Text Based Questions

1. (i) T   (ii) F   (iii) T   (iv) F   (v) T

Language Based Questions

1. (i) (c)   (ii) (d)   (iii) (e)   (iv) (b)   (v) (a)

Chapter 2   Who Will Be Ningthou?

Text Based Questions

1. (i) T   (ii) F   (iii) T   (iv) F   (v) F

Language Based Questions

1. (i) hush   (ii) peck   (iii) crane

[Grammar]

Chapter 1   Articles

1. (i) An   (ii) an   (iii) The   (iv) a   (v) a
2. (i) a   (ii) The   (iii) an   (iv) a   (v) a
   (vi) An   (vii) a   (viii) a   (ix) the   (x) a
3. (i) A   (ii) an   (iii) a   (iv) An   (v) a
4. (i) ☹   (ii) ☺   (iii) ☹   (iv) ☺   (v) ☹

Chapter 2   Nouns and Pronouns

1. **Common Noun** Car, President, Soldier, Doctor, Toothpaste, Dog, Father-in-law, Police station, Capital, Niece, Chocolate

   Proper Noun Rohan, Google, Maruti, Dr Sunanda, Closeup, Vasant Kunj, Bunty, Cadbury, Esselworld

2. (i) cloud   (ii) album   (iii) bunch   (iv) pack   (v) board   (vi) regiment
   (vii) army   (viii) crew   (ix) litter   (x) wad
3. (ii) Puppies   (iii) Thieves   (iv) Judge   (v) Cows   (vi) Calves   (vii) Chocolate
   (viii) Cities   (ix) Town   (x) Countries
4. (i) Aunt   (ii) Queen   (iii) Governor   (iv) Son-in-law (v) Niece   (vi) Hostess
   (vii) Sir   (viii) Shepherdess   (ix) Waitress, (x) Hero   (xi) Widow
   (xii) Countess
5. (i) (c)   (ii) (d)   (iii) (a)   (iv) (d)   (v) (c)

Chapter 3   Conjunctions

1. (i) but   (ii) and   (iii) if   (iv) and   (v) because
2. (i) Radha is dancing and Rashmi is skipping. (ii) Ice is cold but fire is hot.
   (iii) Sujay and Sakshi went to the bank.   (iv) Akash goes to school but Aradhya stays at home.
   (v) Rama is poor but honest.

3. (i) because   (ii) When   (iii) Since   (iv) for   (v) As   (vi) while

4. (i) Incorrect
   The correct sentence is 'Rajiv is poor but honest.'

   (ii) Correct
   This sentence is correct.

   (iii) Incorrect
   The correct sentence is 'We waited till the train arrived.'

   (iv) Incorrect
   The correct sentence is 'He failed although he worked hard.'

   (v) Correct
   This sentence is correct.

5. (i) till   (ii) or   (iii) but   (iv) but   (v) if   (vi) or

Chapter 4   Adjectives

1. (i) left-handed, boyish   (ii) soft, silky   (iii) best
   (iv) blue, swift, wooden, rotten, angry   (v) young

2. quick, brown, lazy, drawing, old, angry

3. (i) Faster, Fastest (ii) Close, Closest (iii) Good, Better   (iv) More, Most
   (v) Thin, Thinnest   (vi) Lengthier, Lengthiest
   (vii) More careful, Most careful   (viii) Bright, Brighter   (ix) Polite, Most polite
   (x) Busy, Busiest

Chapter 5   Prepositions

1. (i) (c)   (ii) (b)   (iii) (c)   (iv) (d)   (v) (c)

2.

Incorrect	Correct
(i) on	into
(ii) with	from
(iii) onto	over
(iv) of	about
(v) on	in

3. (i) to   (ii) on   (iii) in   (iv) for   (v) in
   (vi) in   (vii) for   (viii) on   (ix) for   (x) with

4. (i) across   (ii) under   (iii) on   (iv) about   (v) with
   (vi) of   (vii) of   (viii) at   (ix) with   (x) to

5. (i) In, in   (ii) on   (iii) in   (iv) at, at   (v) on

Chapter 6   Tenses

1. (i) Present Tense (ii) Future Tense   (iii) Past Tense   (iv) Present Tense   (v) Present Tense

2. (i) displayed   (ii) raining   (iii) play   (iv) will go   (v) do

3. (i) I was doing this.   (ii) They were playing there.
   (iii) Ram was at the zoo.   (iv) Tanuj played the guitar.
   (v) Rashmi visited her parents.

4. (i) I will play in the park.   (ii) He will be coming to my home.
   (iii) I will splash water on my face.   (iv) Rahul will play in the park.
   (v) Navneet will be riding a cycle.

5. (i) Hitesh sold his bike on Quikr. (Past)

    (ii) Abdul Kalam was an amazing person. (Past)

    (iii) I met him at the Metro station. (Past)

    (iv) I am reading the book now. (Present continuous)

    (v) We will go there tomorrow to meet him. (Future)

    (vi) Can you take this chair, please? (Present)

6. (i) Steal   (ii) Buy   (iii) Eat   (iv) Blow   (v) Bite

    (vi) Flop   (vii) Chide   (viii) Hide

Chapter 7   Verbs

1. (i) stole   (ii) met   (iii) cooked   (iv) saw   (v) watered, pruned

2. (i) ✗   (ii) ✓   (iii) ✗   (iv) ✗   (v) ✗   (vi) ✗

    (vii) ✓   (viii) ✓   (ix) ✗   (x) ✓

3. (i) can   (ii) May   (iii) could   (iv) should   (v) may

4. (i) gave   (ii) caught   (iii) rises   (iv) went   (v) goes

Chapter 8   Adverbs

1. (i) quickly   (ii) very   (iii) quite   (iv) seldom   (v) often   (vi) immediately

    (vii) forward   (viii) twice   (ix) nearly   (x) How   (xi) slowly, beautifully

2. (i) outside   (ii) once   (iii) bravely   (iv) Why   (v) very   (vi) entirely

4. (i) quickly   (ii) quiet   (iii) happily   (iv) beautifully   (v) well   (vi) loud

Chapter 9   Sentences

1. (i) **Subject** Raman

    Predicate went into the class.

    (ii) **Subject** He

    Predicate is a clever and dishonest man.

    (iii) **Subject** You

    Predicate come at once.

    (iv) **Subject** We

    Predicate came together.

    (v) **Subject** The Himalayas

    Predicate are located in Northern India.

    (vi) **Subject** The poor guy

    Predicate went home without food.

2. (i) (b)   (ii) (e)   (iii) (d)   (iv) (c)   (v) (a)

3. (i) Imperative Sentence   (ii) Exclamatory Sentence

    (iii) Declarative Sentence   (iv) Interrogative Sentence

    (v) Exclamatory Sentence

4. (i) Who has stolen my jacket?   (ii) What is the colour of Simran's coat?

    (iii) Where did you keep the notebook?

    (iv) Where did you go?   (v) How many people went to the party?

5. (i) Sunita has been in the hospital since 10 o'clock.   (ii) Sunday is the first day of the week.

    (iii) Navin, Sheetal and I went to the hotel.   (iv) We came here last night.

    (v) May I have that pen?

Worksheet 1

1. I. (i) (c)   (ii) (b)   (iii) (a)

   III. (i) backward   (ii) minor

2. I. (a)

Worksheet 2

1. I. (i) (c)   (ii) (d)   (iii) (a)

   III. (i) Encouraged   (ii) Litter   (iii) Active

2. I. (i) (d)   (ii) (c)

   III. (i) Feline   (ii) Pupil

Worksheet 3

1. I. (i) (c)   (ii) (c)   (iii) (b)

   III. (i) Real   (ii) Failure

   IV. (i) DISNEY   (ii) ANNUAL

   V. (i) Famous   (ii) Innovator

2. II. (i) Dirty, dirty-faced, dark, horrible, big, lost, sweet, more (any three)

   (ii) Jeremy, Navajo (any one)

   (iii) get, crawling, biting, chewing, digging, peeking, painting, playing, signing, rolling, giving, finding, eating, wrestling, having (any three)

   III. (i) Found   (ii) Clean   (iii) Sour